KE

OON OF

UARE
ORD
by
NGTHS

ORDS

The cry Awwk!
is that of the great
Auk. (see catfish).

Kitchener was drowned
at sea by water, and
his country still
wants you. (see fish).

King Edward the
seventh is enough.

£2·25

The Milligan Book of Records

The amazing Mrs Rueben Croucher

THE MILLIGAN BOOK OF RECORDS

Games, cartoons and commercials

SPIKE MILLIGAN and Jack Hobbs

M & J Hobbs in association with Michael Joseph

First published in Great Britain in 1975 by M & J Hobbs, 25 Bridge Street, Walton-on-Thames, in association with Michael Joseph Ltd, 52 Bedford Square, London W.C.1. ISBN 0 7181 1377 2. Photoset in Great Britain by Filmtype Services Ltd, Scarborough, printed by Hollen Street Press, Slough, and bound by Dorstel Press, Harlow. Designed by Lawrence Edwards.

Learn about

X Learn about the oldest spot in the Atlantic Ocean!

X The Amazing Mrs. Rueben Croucher!

X The World's most unchopped tree!

Astonishing never before told revelations, folks.
Read about the world's largest rupture; the longest man ever hurled;
and the amazing record for one-man formation dancing non-stop
from London to Glasgow.

Ice cream interval in the middle of the book with pull-out usherette . . .
followed by a selection of Christmas games for the sensible child,
cartoons and commercials.
Reach for your money . . . God Bless You Sir!

P.S. Spike Milligan will hold the record for first reading this book.
WILL YOU HOLD THE RECORD FOR BEING SECOND?
Hurry before you're a has-been.

First parachute descent by a cat

World's largest mushroom

The oldest spot in the Atlantic Ocean.

THE HUMAN BEING

The man who holds the world record
for not saying 'fish'
since his third birthday.

The world's largest liver is 68 ft. long and has never been tamed.

The world's largest rupture weighs 18 lb. $3\frac{1}{4}$ oz.
and is about to go metric.
It is now in the keeping of the National Truss.

The longest man ever buried measured 13 miles 6 ft. 11 ins. There is a difficulty about his exact position. It is thought he may have been folded over.

The world record for tree-sitting by a one-legged man with lion is one week— Following this the man was eaten and the lion went on to establish a solo record of 3 weeks and one hour exactly.

World's tallest idiot.

First successful mass hanging – Neasden 1603.

First unsuccessful mass hanging – Neasden 1603.

Pontius Kak
of Scraggs, Notts.
who, when questioned by the police,
said: 'It's the nasturtiums.'

Ed. note: This is the only time such
a reply has ever been recorded
at a police station
– a new international record.

World Record for Airborne Dandruff
held by Mrs Sponaker and
daughter

Colington Blench
is the world's
fastest mango.

The world's largest organ
is hanging
under an elephant in Africa
—see Cook's Tours.

The world's fastest overland lifeboat

The world's record bigamist
is Mr. Snailcroft-Queer.
Two marriages in 4 days and 3 nights.

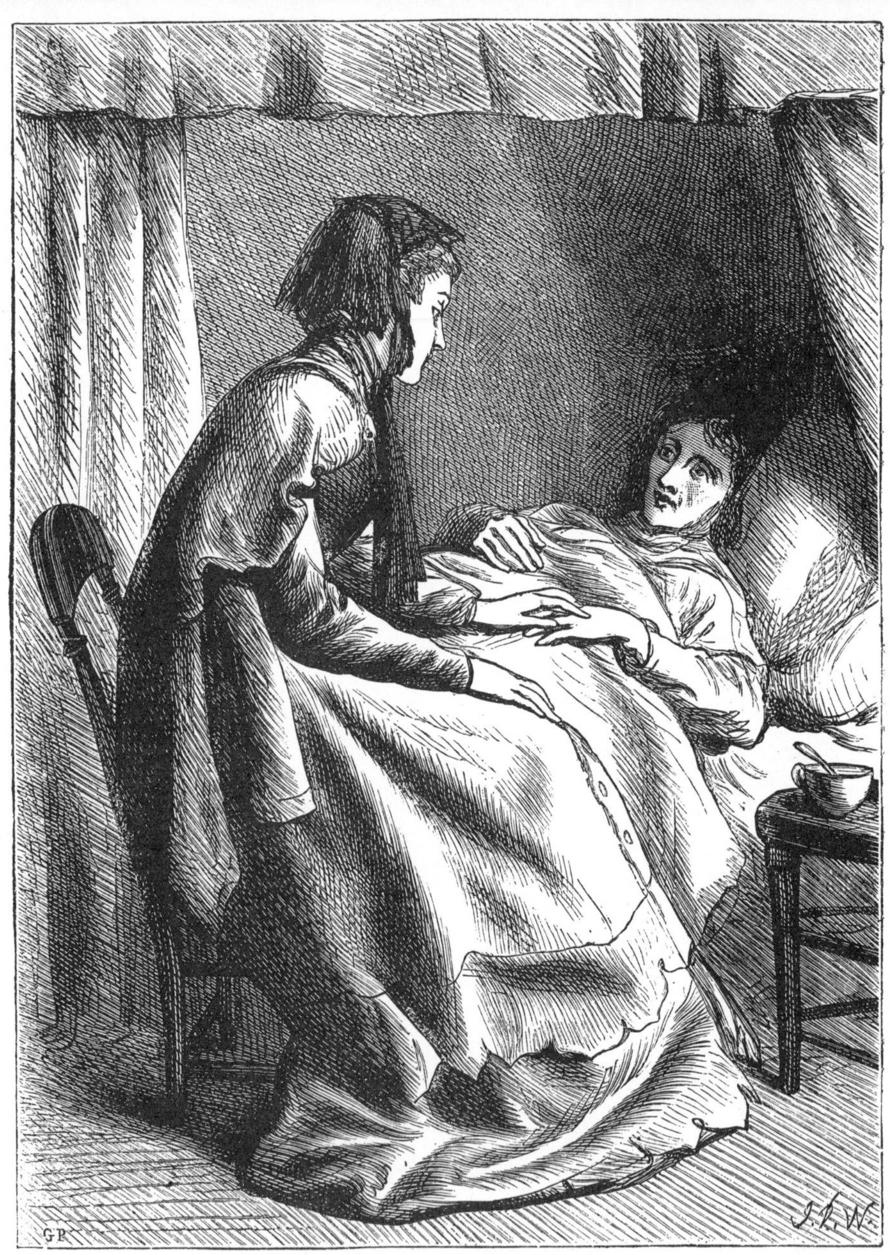

The world's longest deathbed speech – 93 years 2 days 4 hours 3 minutes.

The world's record conversation with a chair goes to Pat O'Rourke – 36 hours 15 minutes.

The world's record for boring children's stories held by Denis Worzel, a deaf yokel.

Animals and Plants

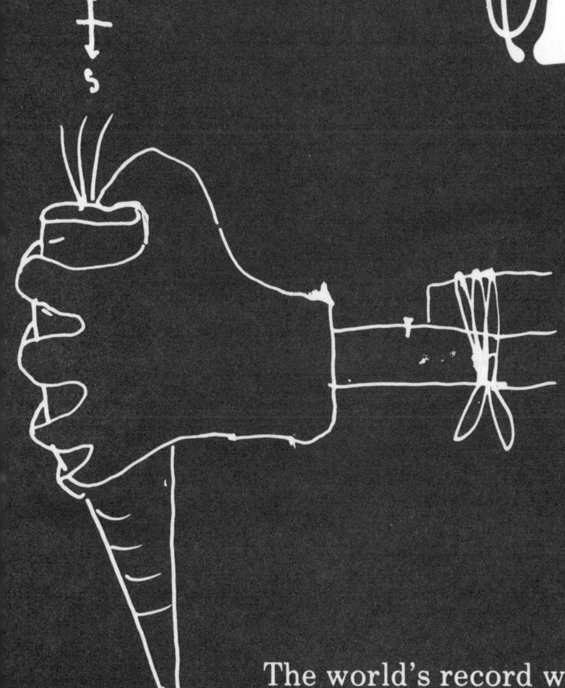

The world's record way to hold a carrot.

THE ONLY NAMELESS HORSE.

The World's most unchopped tree.

Some of the people who have not chopped it down

THE NATURAL WORLD

A picture of the hottest April 6th in West Hartlepool for four hundred years. By a local artist.

Some well-known records:

The 102nd dalmatian

The highest piece of sky is in the region of 439675 depending on waft.

The hottest piece of the sun.

The world's longest fish is Eric Tongs.

The world's largest straight line is between New Zealand and Paraguay except during equinoxes.

Alfred Scraunch has held an unbroken rib-cage for 60 years.

The world's longest mile is $2\frac{1}{2}$ miles long.

The longest nail is in Afghanistan.

The smallest figure quoted on the Stock Exchange floor belongs to Mary – an apprentice lift-girl from Tooting.

The first dog-powered sewing machine

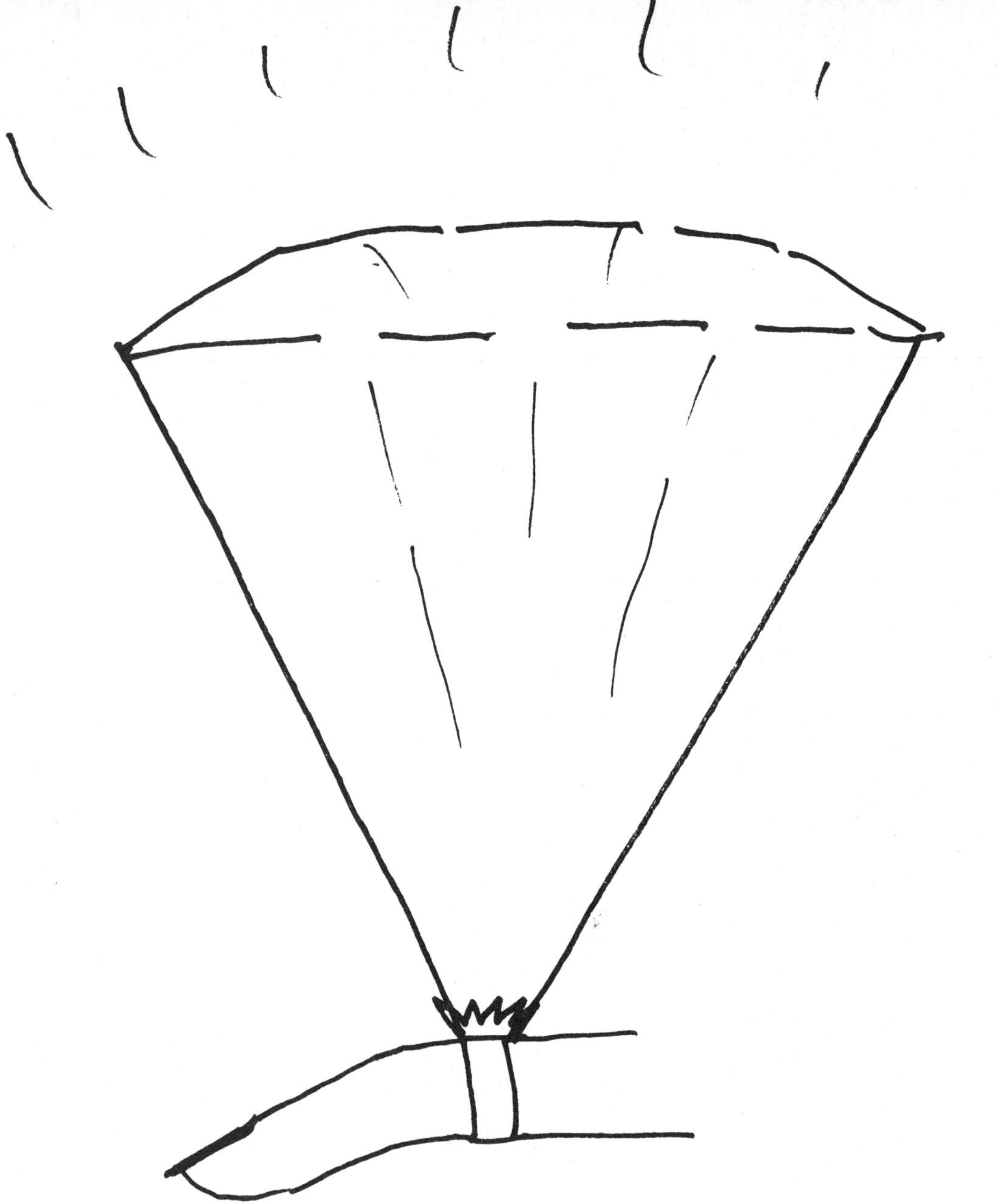

The world's largest diamond.

UNIVERSE & SPACE

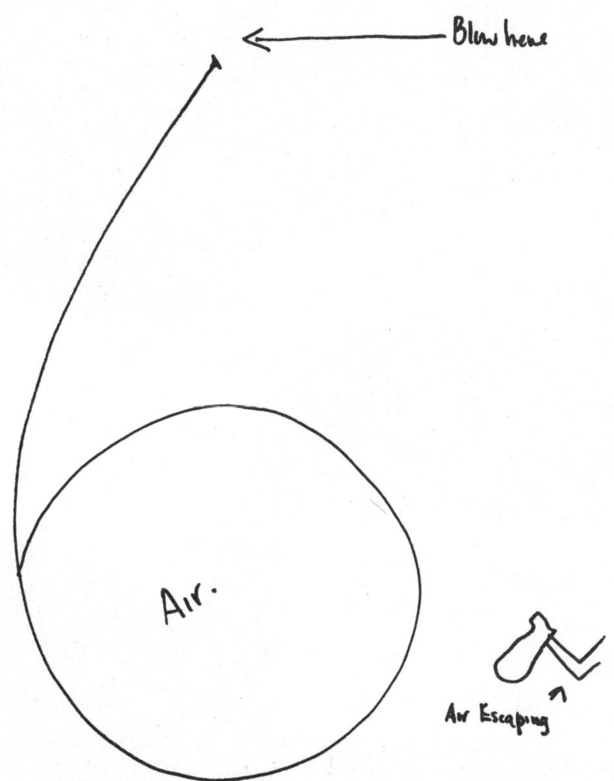

The record for air is six (6).

The Scientific World

The record one-foot rule is $13\frac{1}{4}$ ins. long.

The world's record record is a 58 lb. piece of mahogany with milled edges.

The title for the hottest leap year for a thousand years is held by Gladys Peewitt, a Mormon from Crouch End.

Harrington Pith—the first man able to sing through his earholes—shown in the act of being recorded.

The world's first self-rupture appliance

The world's lowest flying man-powered aircraft. Water-borne aeroplane showing original water.

FAMOUS HOLES

Coal hole near Buckingham Palace.

Buckingham Palace near a coal hole.

FAMOUS HOLES (CONTD.)

BLACK HOLE OF CALCUTTA

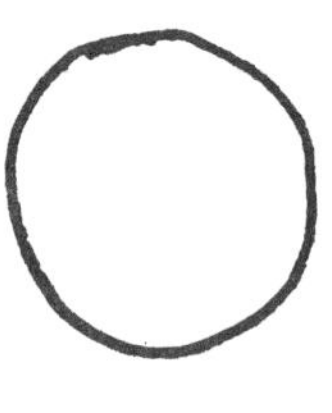

WHITE HOLE OF CALCUTTA

COAL HOLE OF CALCUTTA

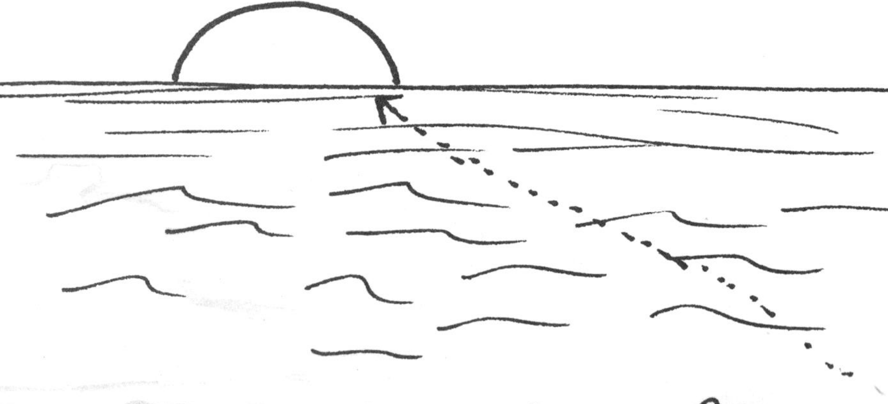

HOLE RISING OVER OLDEST PART OF ATLANTIC OCEAN

The Arts and Entertainment

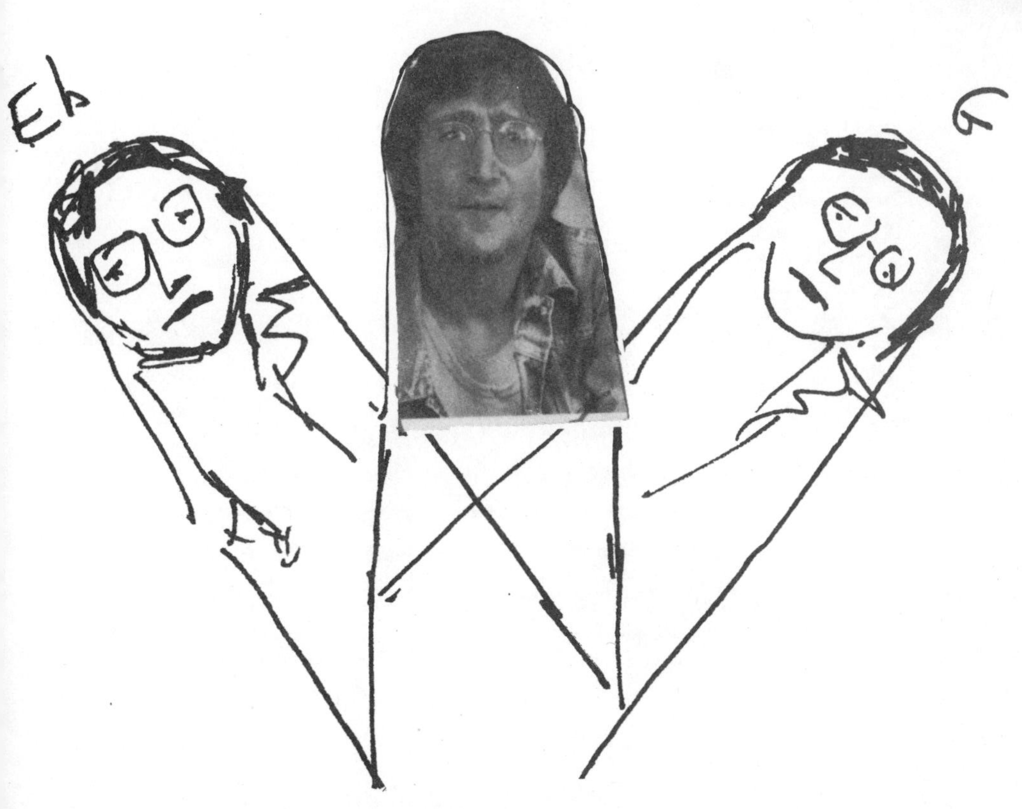

A variable pitch – John Lennon.

Charles Plukk
holds the record
for one-man formation
dancing non-stop
from London to Glasgow.

The world's record
for Ronnie Scott
is held by Ronnie Scott.

STILL TO BE VERIFIED:—
Captain Hugh Cobalt in a submarine
holds the record for singing 'Shadow of your Smile'
in Eb in the *Nautilus* 200 ft.
below the Polar Ice Cap
– mean average temp. –4°;
inside leg 32 ins.

TWO RECORD PLAYERS

JIMMY YOUNG

JIMMY OLD

The greatest number of skaters ever jumped by a barrel is $35\frac{1}{2}$ – the half being a one-legged skater from Ohio who had lost a limb in a previous attempt.

Duke Ellington. His orchestra playing East St. Louis Toodle Oo is also a record.

Another record.

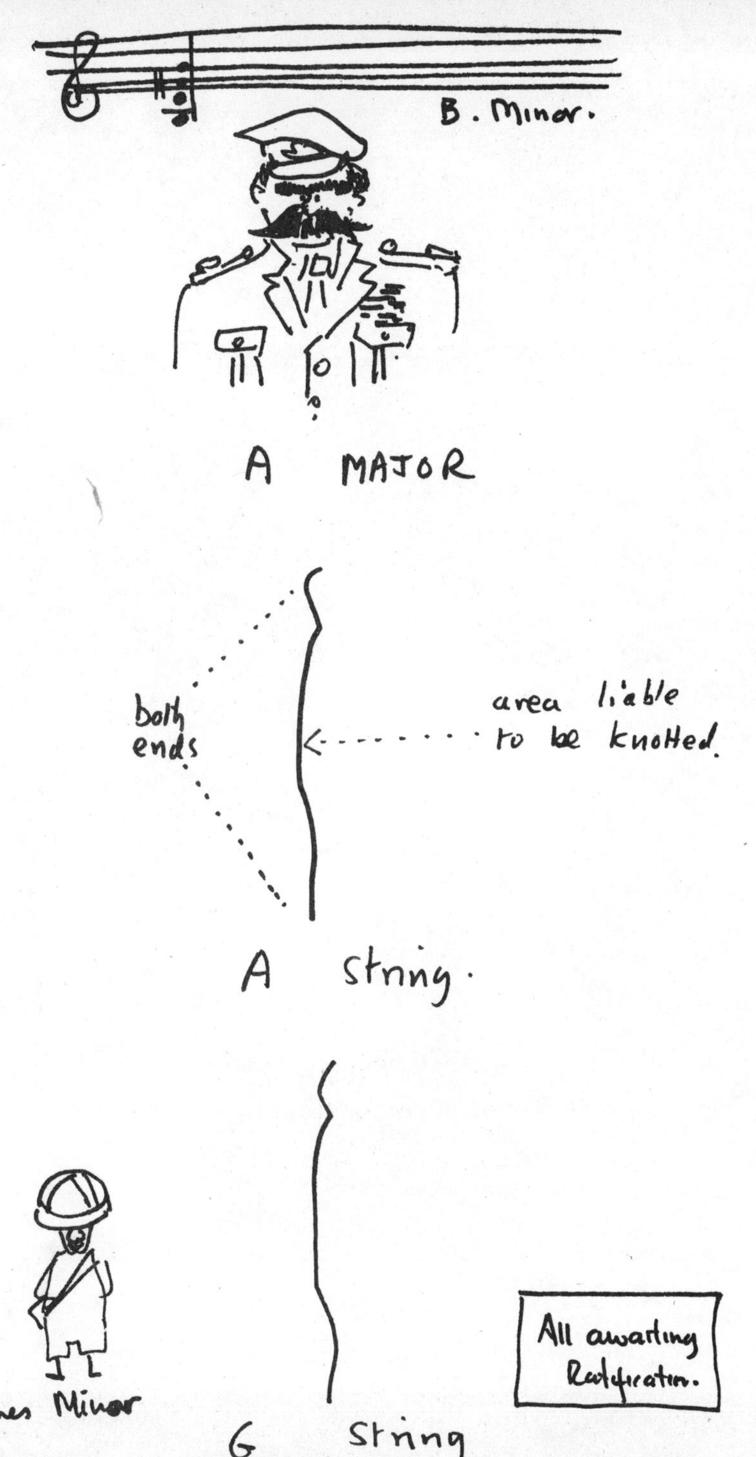
B. Minor.
A MAJOR
both ends
area liable to be knotted.
A string.
Jones Minor
All awaiting Ratification.
G string

The world record
for listening is held by Mrs. Jay Christie.

SPORTS GAMES & PASTIMES

Flavius Grippe
is the holder
of the World's Fruit Cup.

Measure out 100 metres in a straight line
or failing this draw the distance
in a series of rectangles
on the floor of your front room.
Put on running kit
– assume crouching position –
– assume crouching position –
fire gun and set off.
If you get to the finish
before Jessie Owens it is a record.

The world's highest jumper.

The world's record time
for unscrewing an arm held
by Mr. Harcourt de Vere of Penge.
Time 4 seconds.

The world's record free-style drowning
held by Mrs. Doris Romper
taking two days in all,
with only one hour for refreshment.

The world's record for a boat race with only one competitor is held by the man in the boat. Awaiting ratification.

The world's record for pulling off an arm
is held by Mr. Jake Thirsk.
Time – the present.

The world record for balancing a hedgehog on his head is held by a French gipsy with investments in porcelainware.

The world's record for a flea-spotting contest is held by Mr. Joseph Malt – a bloody fool from Reigate.

The world's record for the tallest wave is held by Mlle. Fiti La Ponk. Eiffel Tower 1834.

The world record
holder for blowing
a bugle whilst riding a
bike up-hill, dragging 4.cwt.
of pig-iron and holding his
breath at the same time
is buried at
Blue Lawns Cemetery
Sheffield
North

A selection of famous

ands

'slings AND arrows.....' Shakespeare

'AND he begat.......' The Bible

'AND dances with the daffodils' Wordsworth

John Lennon AND Yoko Ono

'Wages AND Incomes....' Ted Heath. Harold Wilson. Jack Jones; Vic Feather. Clive Jenkins HUGH SCANLON

'My Husband AND I....' H.M. The Queen

The King AND I. Deborah Kerr.

These 'ANDS' are the only ones quoted in this book from the above famous sources.

And now .... David Nixon

And Goodbye Richard Nixon

'And me the 'ammer. A Carpenter.

TALLEST PEER

WORLD'S SHORTEST PIER

RECORD OFFER

A RESINOUS OBJECT OF UNKNOWN AGE

ABOUT A.D. 600.

available in various sizes.

along with free pregnancy test.

see attached notice

↓

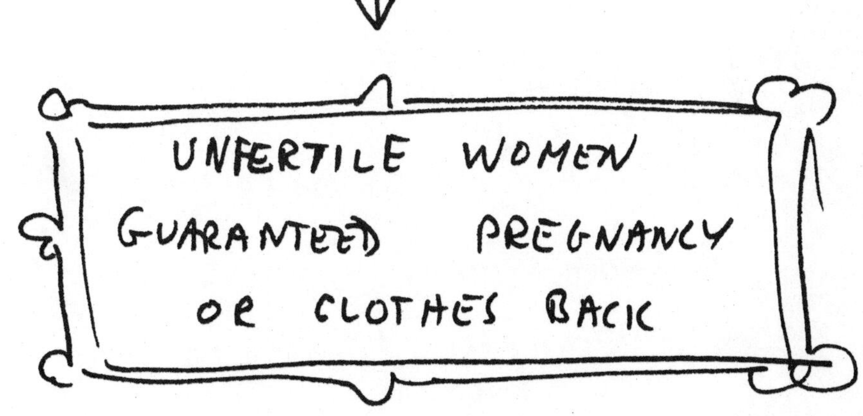
UNFERTILE WOMEN
GUARANTEED PREGNANCY
OR CLOTHES BACK

ed. note

monitor :- UNIQUE RESIN AND PREGNANCY INC.

N.Y.C. N.Y USA

Other first time record quotes:

'£24,640.56 . . .'

'It's the exact distance between two trees – 16 ft. 11$\frac{3}{4}$ ins. . . .'

The world's most exclusive quote: '£1,000,000 with 0.2 pairs of trousers.'

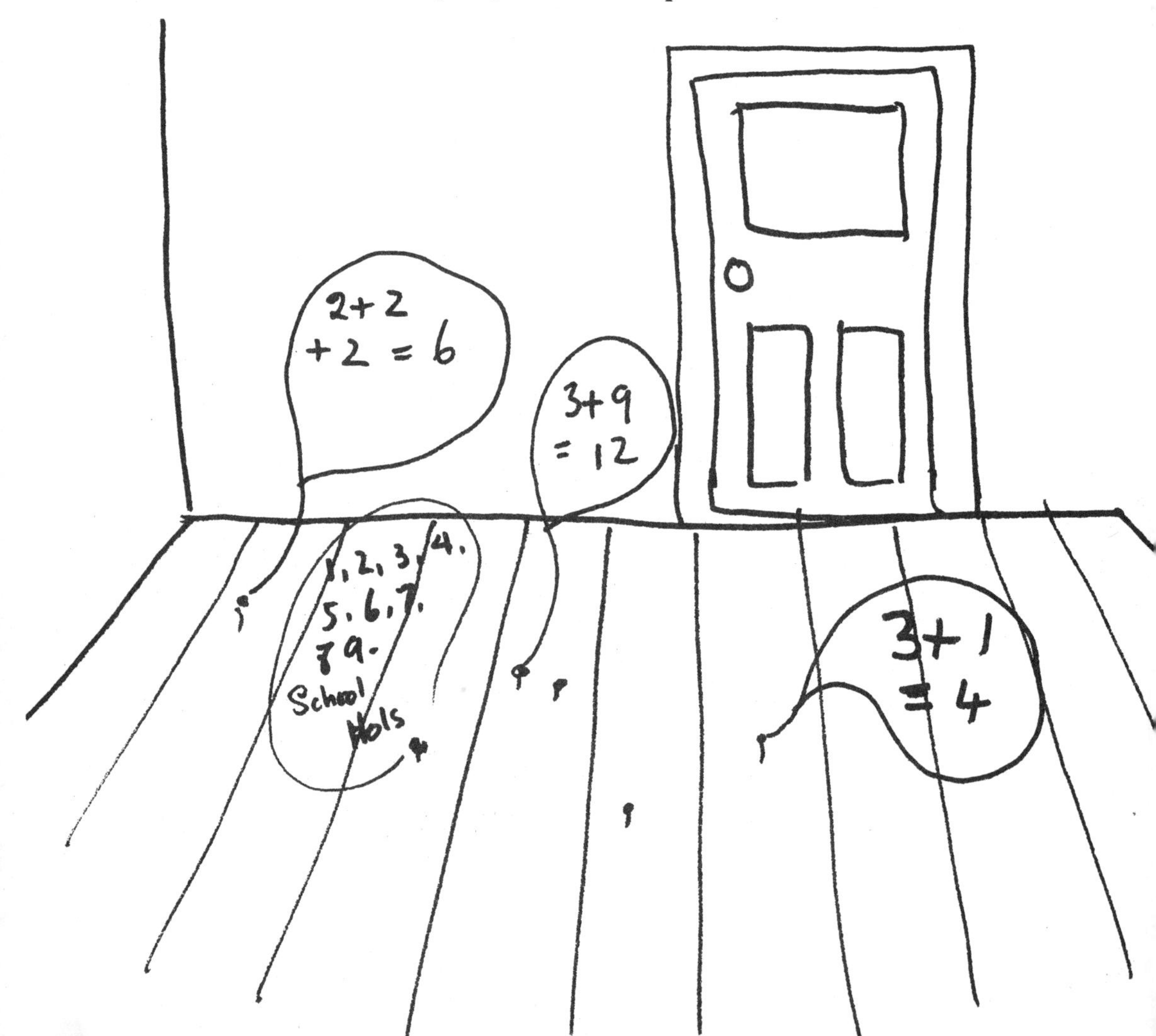

'It's the little things that count.'

With FREE usherette !!

ICES

Obtainable from your nearest chemist, or privately packed and post free at this price from

Shadforth Prescription Service, Ltd. (Dept. PP), 49, King William Street, London, E.C.4.

BEAUTIFUL EYES WIN LOVE!

Richard Tauber & Diana Napier in Capitol Film Production "Land Without Music."

Don't let other girls win all the favours. You, too, can have alluring eyes that coax and thrill the man you want — eyes that are framed in rich, long, lustrous lashes. It's so quick, so easy to do. With a touch of Delica-Brow, Hollywood's long-kept secret, beautiful eyes can now be yours. Delica-Brow is water-proof — in cake or liquid form — in black, brown, or blue, 6d.

Made and Guaranteed by Kissproof Ltd.

Delica-Brow

BE TALLER! Inches Put You Miles Ahead

Increased my own height to 6ft. 3⅜ins.

Ross System Never Fails

Full details 6d. stamp or Complete System £2 2s. Mailed privately in plain cover.

P. MALCOLM ROSS, Height Specialist, Scarborough.

FREE TO LADIES

LADIES should write at once for generous FREE SAMPLE of TRIUMPH FEMALE PILLS for all cases of Anaemia, Irregularities, etc. Safe, Sure, Speedy. To prove these complaints CAN BE CURED write for FREE SAMPLE (post free). sufficient for a cure. Obtainable from Chemists. prices 1/3, 3/-, 5/- and 12/-.

THE MANAGERESS, LE BRASSEUR SURGICAL CO., LTD. (Dept. H.M.), 90 WORCESTER STREET, BIRMINGHAM.

A PERFECT BUST

MAGNETIC CURVES—YOURS IN 4 WEEKS
THREE DIFFERENT TREATMENTS

DEVELOPING FORMOSA CREAM

This truly amazing harmless Cream will positively develop the bust as much as **1½ inches in a week, easily**. Simply apply the Cream to the skin at night, and you will be amazed at the results after only a few applications. **Let Formosa Cream** treatment develop your bust as nothing else can. Acquire the magic of a firm, rounded, shapely bust, and you will have that irresistible feminine charm admired by all. Formosa will add firm, healthy flesh to any part of the body, leaving the skin satin smooth. **The full 4 weeks' complete supply of Formosa Cream treatment costs as little as 6s., post free in plain sealed package.**

STRENGTHENING Formosa Lotion

If you have an ugly, flabby, sagging bust, then Formosa Lotion cannot fail to make it firm and high. After only a few applications, you will notice your bust taking on a new charm, losing those ugly flabby, sagging lines that have worried you for years. Simply apply the lotion to the skin at night, and in a **few weeks** you will have those fascinating curves which are woman's greatest source of attraction. Formosa Lotion tones up and tightens the muscles of the bust, at the same time acting as a tonic for the skin. It definitely does NOT enlarge the bust. What Formosa Lotion has done for others it can do for you. Do not let an ugly, drooping bust line spoil your feminine allure any longer. Guaranteed harmless. Results permanent. **The full 4 weeks' treatment costs only 10s., post free in plain sealed package.**

REDUCING "FOAM" CREAM

There is no reason why you should have a heavy, oversized bust, when Formosa "FOAM" Cream will remould and reduce it—an inch a week—giving those lovely slender, youthful lines, that ONLY Formosa can give. No matter what you may have used before, Formosa "FOAM" Cream will succeed where all others have failed. Simply apply this wonderful non-greasy reducing preparation to the skin, and you will be amazed at the results within a few days. Pleasant to use, Formosa "FOAM" Cream treatment is a tonic for the skin, and will definitely reduce the bust, and any part of the body, leaving the skin satin smooth and refreshed. Results permanent. Absolutely harmless. Failure impossible. **The full 4 weeks' treatment is sent privately in plain sealed package, post free. Price 10s.**

TESTIMONIALS

Miss N. L. T. writes: "After using your Formosa Cream, I developed my bust almost 5 inches. I might mention that I have tried several other preparations without any success." Mrs. J. W. writes: "Your treatment for making the bust firm is simply marvellous. Really, I thought it was impossible for my bust to go back to its normal position." Miss L. B.: "I have reduced my bust 3 inches by using your Foam Cream. Please send me another supply to use on my ankles."

GUARANTEE

If you are not satisfied with Formosa Preparations, your money will be refunded in full

FORMOSA PREPARATIONS

SEND TO-DAY

If you have no ice cream in the house
– here is a list of shops that don't sell it.

FORDS OF DAGENHAM

THE ALBERT HALL

CHELSEA FIRE STATION

HENDON TOWN HALL

INTERFLORA

AMERICAN EXPRESS

DINERS CLUB

ST. PAULS

SCOTLAND YARD

And your life line says you're going to kick the bucket any minute now.

A NON PULL-OUT CARTOON SUPPLEMENT

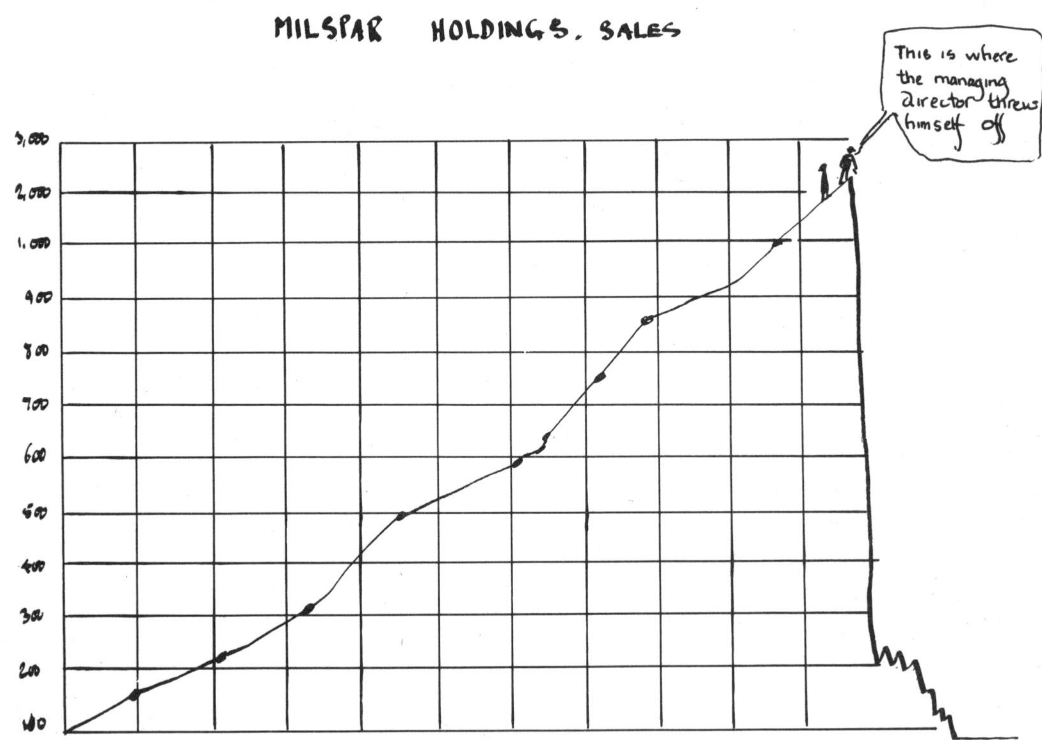
MILSPAR HOLDINGS. SALES
This is where the managing director threw himself off
3,000
2,000
1,000
900
800
700
600
500
400
300
200
100

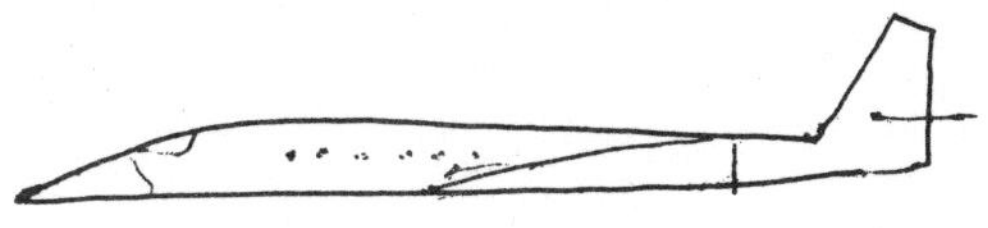
Wat IS THat DAD?
that is a flying Ground nut Scheme Son
S. Morgan

X RAY ROOM

X-
ROOM
S. Milligan

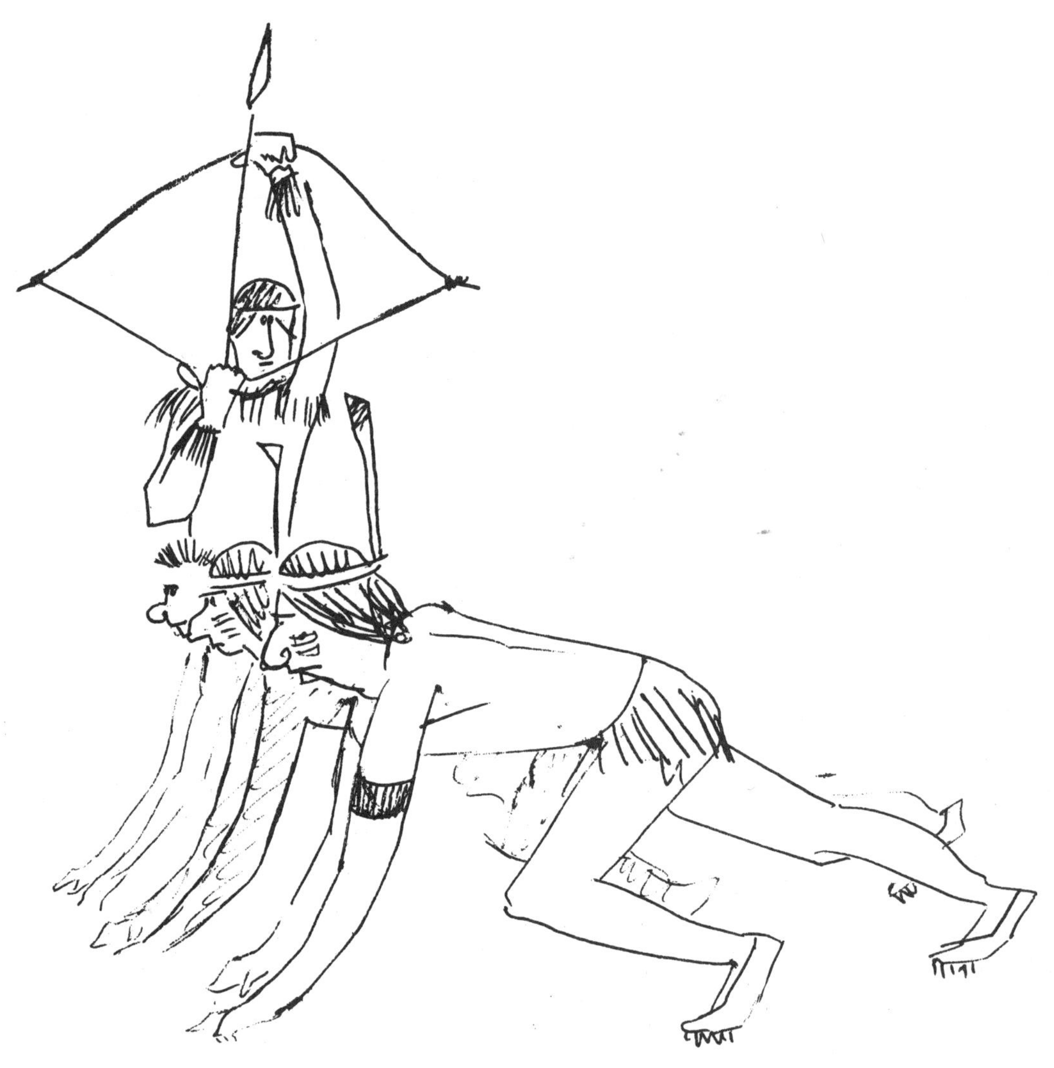

They say he was a contortionist and he died in the middle of a trick.

1
2
3

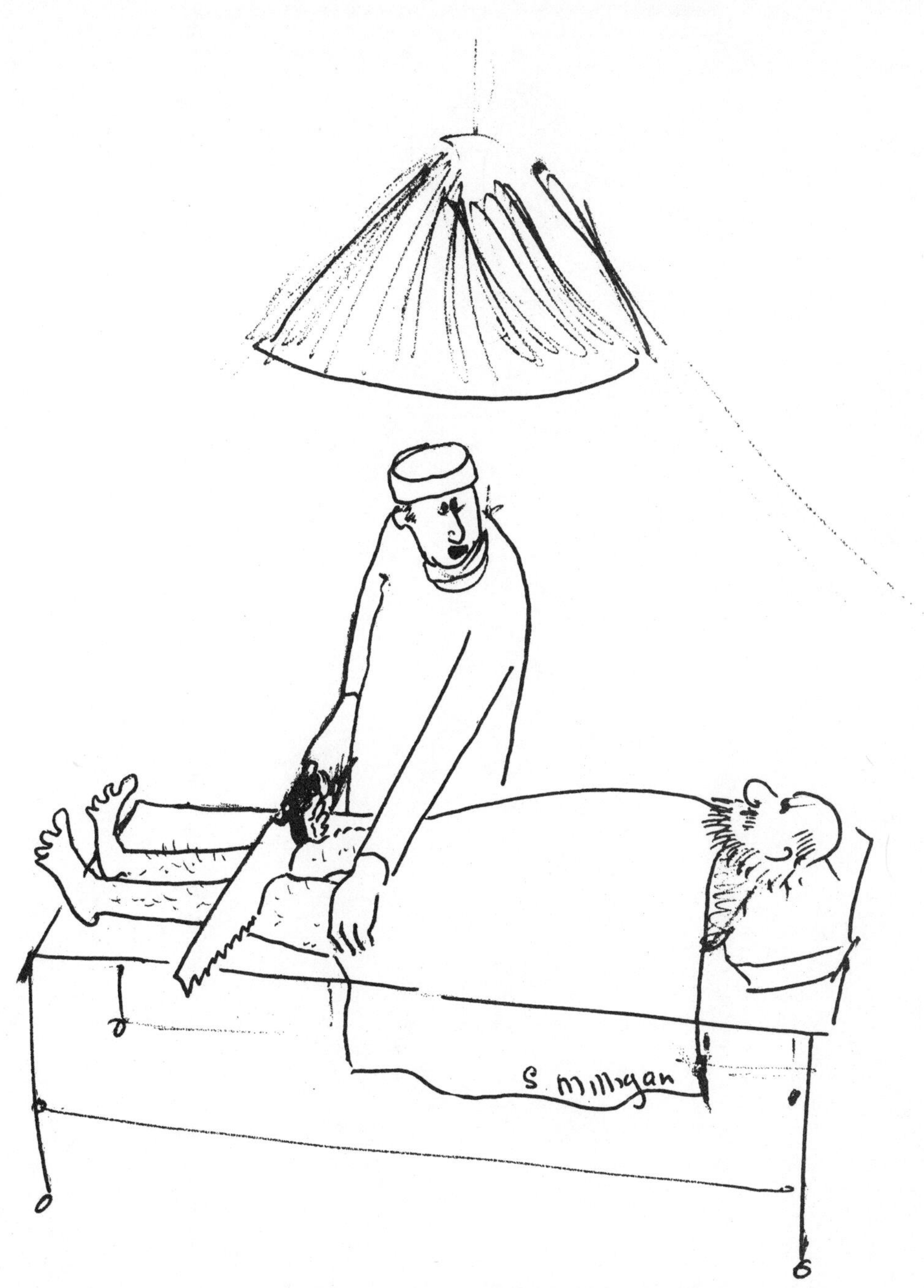

Of course this doesn't necessarily mean you'll paint like Toulouse-Lautrec.

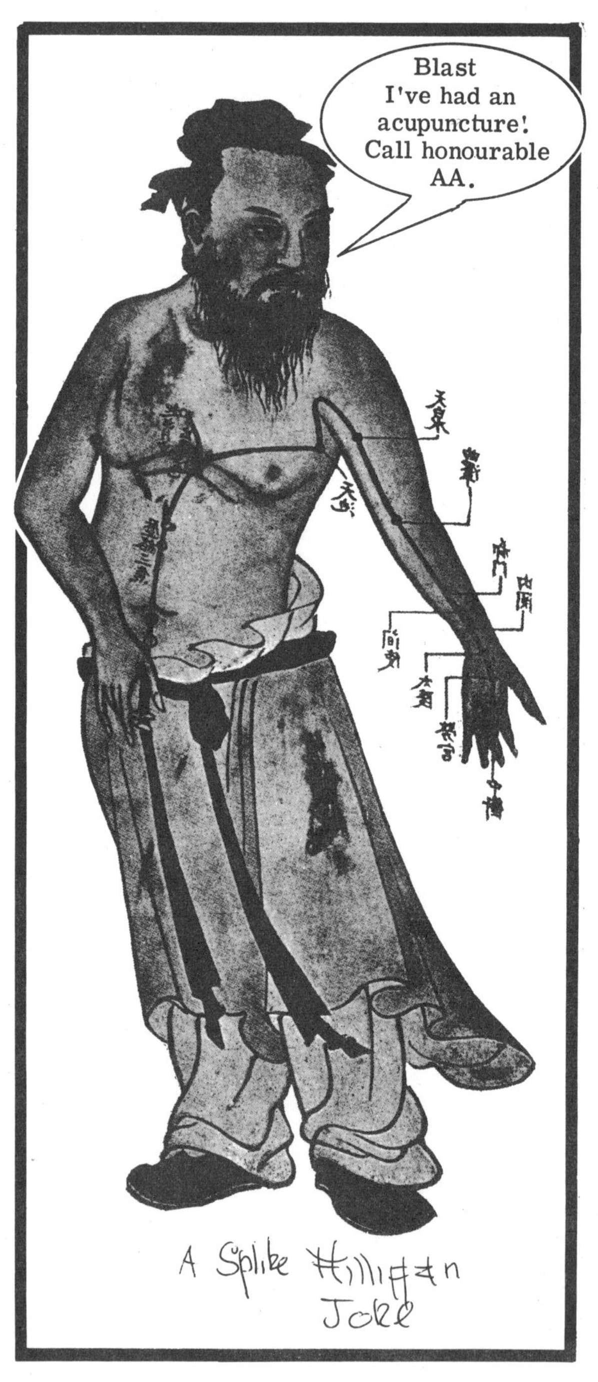
Blast
I've had an
acupuncture!
Call honourable
AA.
A Spike Milligan
Joke

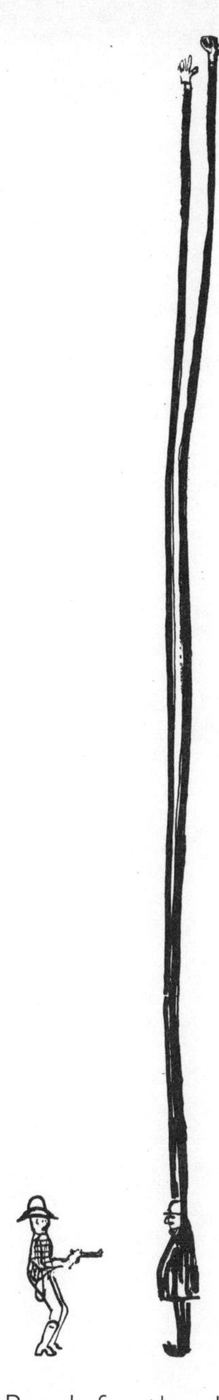

Reach for the sky.

S. Milligan

"It looks like a booby trap sir"

A Spike Milligan
World War II Joke

"Anyone hurt?"

LOOK, ONE MORE CHORUS AND YOU REALLY MUST GO.
Yours etc
Jim

11.15 P.M

I TELL YOU IT WON'T WORK WITH CLOTHES ON.
Yours Sincerely Ethyl

ALL MY OWN WORK
S Milligan

Hands up! I said.

When I said disguise yourself – !

A JOKE BY SPIKE MILLIGAN

Leonardo D. Milligan

HOW are you Mr. Tailor?!
Please dont shout

Spike Milligan

Hurry up!
- I'm waiting to go.

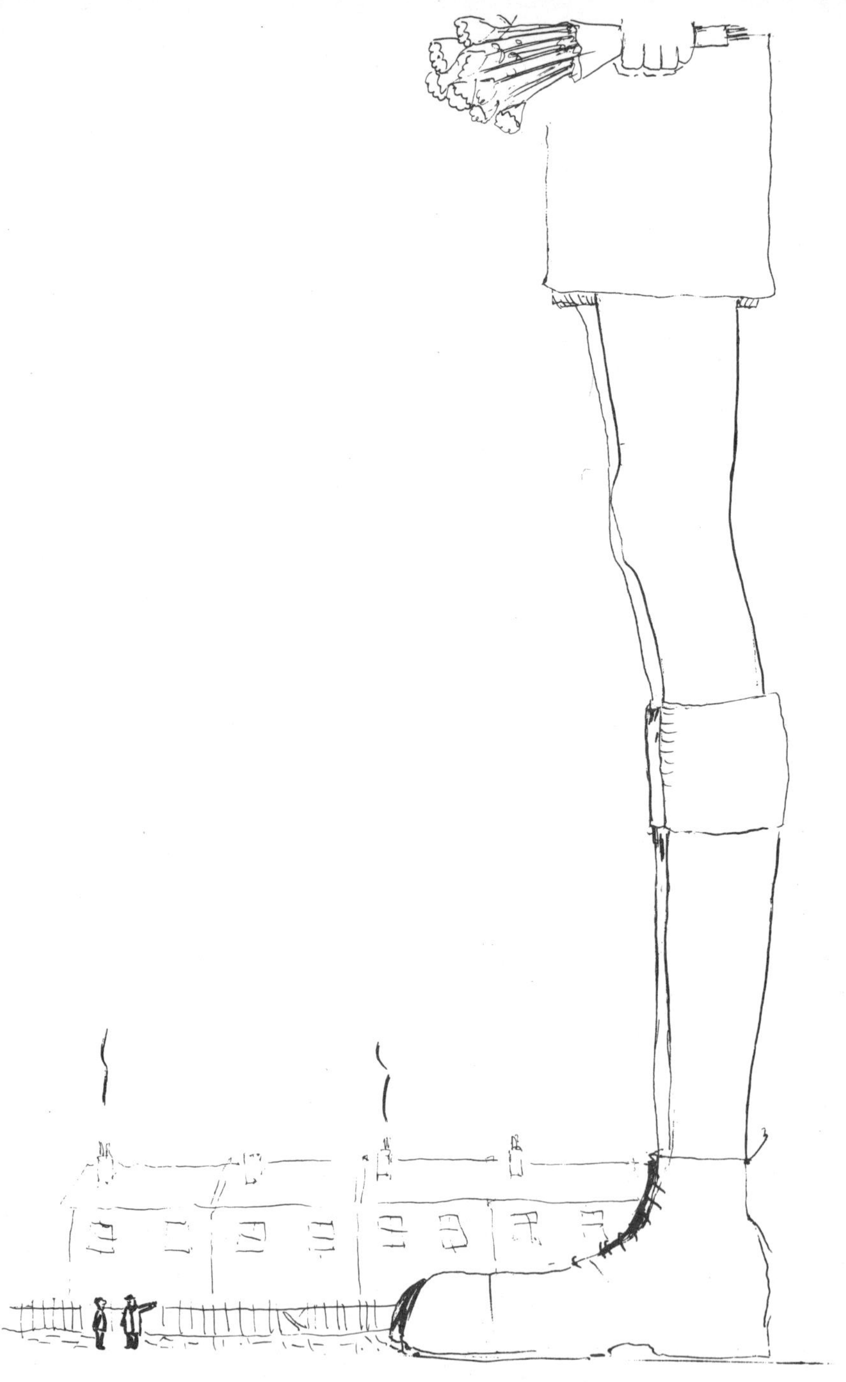

I don't care about his glands. I'm not having him hanging around my daughter.

NO SIGNALS.
BLIND DRIVER.
GLX 391½

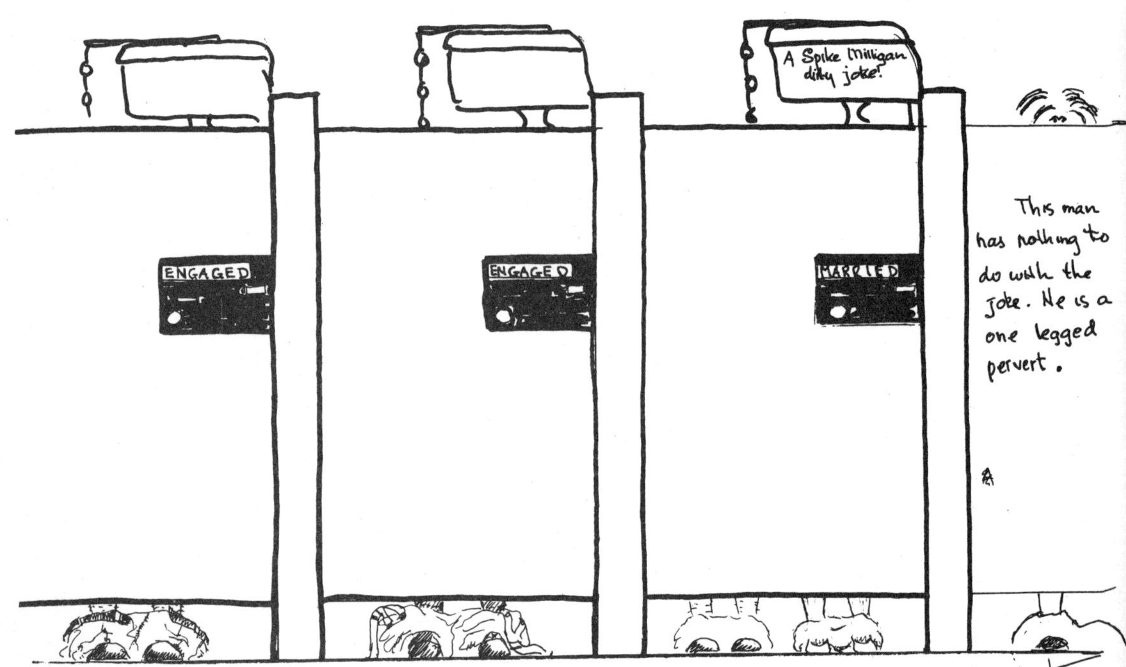
A Spike Milligan dirty joke!
ENGAGED
ENGAGED
MARRIED
This man has nothing to do with the joke. He is a one legged pervert.

A sensible child's guide to Christmas games

Game One:

THE ESCAPE GAME

Tell mummy and daddy and all the family to come into the front parlour. If they are already in there – don't.

For this game you will need the following:

A Six Inch Nail
A Hammer
A Piece of String.

Having got these you then ask all the family to go out of the parlour. You tell them they mustn't come in until you shout READY. Now, hammer the six inch nail into the parlour wall. Tie one end of the string round the nail and the other end round your neck. Next strike one of the matches. Hold the flame underneath the string until it burns through. Then shout READY.

When the family come in you say "Look Mummy I'm free".

Game Two:

HIDING

For this game you will need a Grandad.

For this game you will need:

A Grandfather

A Chest in the Hall.

The game is, you have to hide grandfather. Then the family have to look for him. On no account must you tell them where he is. That would be cheating.

Send all the family into another room. Then take grandfather to the chest in the hall. Ask him to get in. When he has done this you carefully lock and bolt the chest and hide the key. Go back into the parlour and shout READY.

In they must come and start looking everywhere in the room. After a long time they will say "We give up, where is he?" And you say "I'm sorry I can't tell you. That would spoil the game". If by next Christmas they haven't found him, you must say "It's no good I can't keep him secret any longer, he's in the chest in the hall".

Ask Grandad, has he ever seen the inside of the chest in the hall?

The rest of the family should go in the next room and wait.

When they ask you where Grandad is tell them you can't say as it will spoil the game.

Game Three:

STOP-A GRANNY

For this game Granny must get out of bed and come down into the parlour. (The older the granny the greater the fun).

First get the family to help you to lay Granny on the floor in front of the fire to keep her nice and warm. Now you say "Everybody must go outside and wait". When they have gone, take a nice heavy velvet cushion and place it gently over Granny's face. Now stand on Granny's arms, sit on the cushion, and count out loud from one to a hundred. Then shout READY. And when they all come into the room you shout "Look Granny's gone".

Get Granny out of bed and ask her to come downstairs.

Game Four:

HITTING

This game is very simple. With a minimum of two players.

You sit facing each other on chairs, someone must play a jolly tune on the piano, and you hit each other in time to the music. Whoever's left wins.

Game Five:

BAIT THE WEAKLING

For this game you need the weakest member of your family (an anaemic cousin would be ideal).

Get a stout rope and ask the weakling to tie it round his neck.

You then say "Wait here," unroll the coil of rope, and carry the other end out of the front door and into a waiting motor car. Make sure that the hood is down so that you can see him when he appears. Get daddy to put the car into first gear. Tell him to increase the speed gradually and keep your eye on the front door. Your daddy will let in the clutch and you must shout READY. As the car moves forward keep your eye on the front door. Soon the weakling will appear and you shout "There he is". The first one to see him gets five points. Your daddy must drive the car at a steady twenty miles an hour as we don't want to overtax the weakling and the game can be spoilt if it ends too quickly. Try and keep the rope taut to keep him moving. If the rope goes slack he gets four points. If he falls and is dragged for more than a hundred yards he loses his points and has to start again. This game can last as long as he does.

When you reach home add up the points. If he wins he should be put to bed with a hot drink and then buried.

Try and keep the rope taut.

Game Six:

HELP THE POOR BEGGAR

or HIDE THE CANDLESTICK

Go out into the street and find a poor beggar. Tell him this is his lucky day. And when you take him home every one will be waiting with a beautiful dinner for him in the lounge. Give him a nice drink of sherry, as strong as possible to help cheer him up and give him a good appetite for his dinner. Then give a little jerk and spill some of the sherry down his shirt front and say "I'm sorry, don't worry it's Christmas". Then try and slip a silver candlestick in his sock. If you do this without drawing his attention you get ten points. Everybody must try and keep him away from the dinner. This gives you five points. Remember every mouthful he eats is four points to him and he could win. Daddy will now come in dressed as a policeman, but just before he does try and put a pair of mummy's knickers in the beggar's hand (this could get you a hundred points). Daddy should then strike him from behind with an iron bar saying "You drunken sex maniac you have stolen my candlestick and you have lost the game", whereupon the whole family pick up the beggar and hurl him through the plate glass window.

I've found somebody to play 'Find the Candle' dear.

Game Seven:

MANGLE ONE TWO

Tell the family to go into the garden with shovels and wait.

MANGLE THREE

For this you need two players, you and somebody else. Children usually play it with uncles.

Wait till after Christmas lunch when uncle is asleep by the fire.

Get a nice cotton wool ball and soak it with chloroform. Put it neatly on uncle's nose. If he wakes up start again. The rest of the family should wait in the garden with shovels.

Then pull his chair towards the mangle in the kitchen all the while saying "Mangle, mangle, one two three" so that people will know it is just a game.

Take off uncle's boots and put them neatly in the fire. Get the ends of his socks in between the rollers of the mangle and start to turn the handle saying "Mangle, mangle, one two three" so that everyone will know it's just a game. And if he wakes up tell HIM it's only a game but turn the handle quicker as you haven't got long to go. Later slide him under auntie's door chanting "MANGLE, mangle, one two three" to show her it's only a game.

When the police arrive the game is over.

Game Eight:

FIND THE DOGGIE

For this you need a hungry Alsatian and two legs.

First when Daddy is asleep hide all his trousers and underpants. Tell him not to be angry as it is only a game. When he says "How does it go?" blindfold him and tie his hands behind his back. The rest of the family must put on their best clothes and wait in the garden. Take him to the cupboard where the growling is coming from, push him in and shout "FIND THE DOGGIE DADDY".

Then the family must rush in and, to stop the bleeding, tie tourniques above each of Daddy's knees. When the doctor arrives you stop him at the door and tell him "DADDY'S FOUND THE DOGGIE" and the game is over.

Game Nine:

XMAS HOUSEY HOUSEY

For this game you need an expensive house.

If you live in a big expensive house here is a nice Christmas Family Game.

For this game ask Daddy for the deeds of the house. Then all the family must go and hide in the garden. Lock and bolt all doors and windows. Now phone Goldsmith and Howland Estate agents and say "5bd, kt. 2bths, cons., c.h., grg. for 3 crs., 3 recep., full. furn., snip at £50, owner going abroad". When the man arrives, you send Daddy in blindfolded and say sign here. The agent will say "A merry Christmas to you all" and will count out fifty pound notes and say "Who's for this then?". You will snatch the money shouting "House". Daddy must then say "Who's" and Mr. Goldsmith & Howland will say "Mine—now get out".

Soon a man from Goldsmith and Howland will come.

Game Ten:

CARRYING THE CRIPPLE

This is a good Christmas Game.

If you play all the above games correctly and conscientiously by game NINE you should be alone in the house and very rich.

A Merry Christmas to you.

Enter your own DIY records here and keep this book up to date

Example of a DIY record:–
The 103rd Oxo cube used at 7 Cringe Terrace, Bombay

If you run out of space buy another copy

3½" is taller than 2".

Ireland is higher.

Knotted string is valuable if knotted.

Grey hair goes with heads.

Identically different plimsolls are one and the same.

X marks the spot but the spot is greater to the sum of the other two sides.

SP

MILLIG

BUK

A S
R
SU
TOM

RECO

STO